New England's MARVELOUS MONSTERS

This book is dedicated to Allen Janard of Salem, Massachusetts, who doesn't believe in sea monsters — Maybe after reading this, he will.

D1452857

Sketch of the sea serpent "Nellie" off Boston - Courtesy, The Peabody Museum, Salem, MA.

Cover Photos: ISBN-0-916787-02-8

(1) The decaying remains of a sea monster with giant flippers, dredged up from 1,000 feet by a Japanese fishing trawler in 1977- A.P. photo. (2) "The Grand Serpent", a lithograph, courtesy Peabody Museum, Salem, MA. (3) "Old Stormalong" riding a whale, painting, courtesy John Hancock Mutual Life Insurance Co., Boston, MA. (4) The Goosefish, Paul Tzimoulis photo. (5) A ten-foot Nurse Shark, photo by Paul Tzimoulis.

INTRODUCTION

Most people love sea stories and adventures concerning sea monsters, but sea serpents have not yet made it in today's society. A few people may accept their existence, but most scoff at their mere mention. Concrete evidence however, is mounting to establish the existence of sea serpents. Over 1,000 people saw "Nellie", the North Shore sea serpent off the Massachusetts coast back in the 1800's, and that is more than the number who claim to have seen "Nessie" in Loch Ness. Many spot "Champ" in Vermont's largest lake every year— there were 14 sightings in 1985.

New England is ripe with sealore, but I have omitted the legend here and collected only unusual factual stories that are well documented. During my 25 or so years of research, I have made some startling discoveries, such as the macabre fate of all ships given the name ATLANTIC, and the strange coincidence of the number 33 surrounding all New England submarine disasters. I do not try to explain the reasons for any odd occurences; and, I do not attempt to solve the many mysteries presented here— I leave these puzzling incidents for you to wrestle with in your own mind. I have merely collected some stories about local places that I know and love, from New England to Newfoundland. Some of these stories are humorous, others are terrifying, and most boggle the mind. Marvelous Monsters is the third in this classic series of sixteen books.

Bob Cahill

A 55-foot giant squid, stranded in the shallows of New-foundland in 1875, and cast in plaster by scientists of Smithsonian Institution, Washington, D.C., where it is now on display.

I
THE PLUM ISLAND MONSTER

Plum Island, a long sandy extension of Newburyport, Massachusetts, now a penninsula, is a great place to swim and frolic during the summer months. Part of the island is a national bird preserve, and, although there are a few summer cottages and winter homes at the base of the island, miles of beaches and sand-dunes are open to the public for picnicing. In the past 300 years, during storms many old sailing ships have crashed ashore on Plum Island and occassionally, when the wind shifts the dunes, white oaken ribs and beams have been exposed for picnickers to wonder at. In February of 1980, something else crashed ashore at Plum Island, which caused more than wonder. It was a twelve-foot, 450 pound sea monster, still wiggling in its death throes, it's parrot-like beak snapping at anyone who dare approach it. Stretching beyond its twelve-foot bulk, were ten tentacles measuring from 10 to 16-feet in length, that could easily grasp a man around the middle and reel him in to its bone crushing beak. By the time experts from Boston's New England Aquarium arrived, the monster was dead, but with the help of a winch, they scooped the remains up into a truck and transported the beast to the Aquarium. In Boston, it was preserved in ice to await examination from Dr. Clyde Roper, a curator of Smithsonian Institution, who flew into Boston from Washington D.C. He probed it, poked at it, and measured it. The creature, he concluded, was an ocean going squid.

I had seen thousands of baby squid, only a few inches long, swimming in nearby Salem Harbor, but a giant such as this in New England waters? Was it a freak I wondered? No, it wasn't! Doctor Roper set me straight. Not only are giant squid in these waters, but they breed just north of New England waters, off Nova Scotia and Newfoundland. The Plum Island monster was, in fact, small, as compared to other giant squid that have come ashore. Living up to the true meaning of "monsters," they can be extremely dangerous and vicious.

Young Tom Piccot lived on the coast of Conception Bay, Newfoundland, and at age twelve was an accomplished herring fisherman. Every day but Sunday, he would venture out into the bay to fish from a 20-foot dory, with his father and his father's fishing partner. On the morning of October 26, 1873, the three of them had rowed out, set their nets and anchored the dory off the Eastern end of Belle Isle. The water was calm, but the fish didn't seem to be biting too well this day. At 11:00 A.M., as Tom sat in the bow of the small boat daydreaming into the shimmering waters, he saw two huge green eyes staring back at him from the depths. He screamed to the two men that there was a monster under the boat, and their responding smiles were soon washed away when a slimy grey arm, the size of their boat, wiggled its way up from the sea into Tom's father's lap. Then another great arm peppered with suction cups slid over the gunwhales of the boat as Tom and the men watched in horror and disbelief. The huge green eyes and parrot-like beak of the creature broke the surface waters and ten long slithering arms began climbing aboard the dory in an attempt to drag it and its occupants under.

Tom's father struck out at the giant squid with a boat hook, but this seemed only to provoke the creature into a firmer embrace of their boat. The dory began to tip and its seams were cracking under the presure of the creature's 20-foot tentacles. Young Tom Piccot picked up an axe from under the floorboards and smashed at the tentacles. Hacking away furiously, he managed to cut off two of the arms. The sea around them was then clouded with a black inky fluid. The creature released its grip and retreated into the depths. Tom Piccot was the hero of the day--not only did he have the praise of his father and his father's friend because he had slain a great sea monster, but he recovered two 20-foot tentacles to prove to his pals and the local fishermen that his encounter was not just another tall fisherman's tale.

Less than seven months later, another Newfoundlander, William Darling, had an even more terrifying experience with a giant squid. The skipper of the schooner PEARL, James Floyd, reported the incident in the July 5, 1874 issue of "News of the World." His statement is as follows:

"I was lately the skipper of the schooner PEARL, a 150-ton tight little craft with a crew of six men. We were bound from Mauritius to Rangoon, tin ballast to return with padding and had put into Galle for water. Three days out we fell becalmed into the bay, latitude 8 degrees 50 min. N., and longitude 84 degrees 5 min. E. At about 5:00 P.M. we sighted a two-masted steamer on our port quarter, about five or six miles off. Very soon after, as we lay motionless, a great mass rose slowly out of the sea about a half-mile off on our starboad side, and remained spread out and stationary. It looked like the back of a huge whale, but sloped less, and was of a brownish color. Even at that distance it seemed much longer than our craft, and it seemed to be basking in the sun."

"I went into the cabin for my rifle, and, as I was preparing to fire, Bill Darling, a Newfoundlander, came on deck, and looking at the monster exclaimed: 'Have a care, that there's a squid, and will capsize us if we hurt him.' Smiling at the idea, I let fly... hit him and with that he shook. There was a great ripple all around him and he began to move."

"Out with your axes and knives," shouted Bill, "and cut any part of him that comes aboard; look alive and Lord help us."

"Not aware of the danger, and never having seen or heard of such a monster, I gave no orders, and it was no use touching the helm or ropes to get out of the way."

"By this time three of the crew, Bill included, had found axes, and all were looking over the ship's side at the advancing monster. We could see now a large oblong mass moving by jerks, just under the surface of the water, and an enormous train following; the oblong body was at least half the size of our vessel in length, and just as thick; the wake of the train might have been 100 feet long. In the time I have taken to write, the brute struck us, and the ship quivered under its thud; in another moment the monster was aboard, squeezed in between the masts. The brute, holding on by its arms, slipped its vast body overboard and pulled the vessel down with it on her beam ends. Monstrous arms like trees seized the vessel, and she reeled over. We were thrown into the water at once, and just as I went over, I caught sight of one of the crew, either Bill or Tom Fielding, squashed up between the masts in one of those awful arms. For a few seconds our ship lay on her beam ends, then filled and went down. Another of the crew must have been sucked down, for only five of us were picked up."

This statement was signed by James Floyd, late master of the schooner. One of the many passengers on the nearby steamer STRATHOWEN who saw the PEARL go under, gives the following report:

"Steering over a calm and tranquil sea. About an hour before sunset on May 10, we saw, on our starboard beam and about two miles off, a small schooner, lying becalmed. As I examined her with my binoculars, and then noticed between us, but nearer to her, a long, low swelling lying on the sea, which, from its color and shape, I took to be a bank of seaweed. The mass was then set in motion. It struck the schooner, which visibly reeled and then righted. Immediately afterwards, the masts swayed sideways and with my glass I could clearly discern the enormous mass and hull of the schooner coalescing. The other gazers witnessed the same appearance. The schooner's mast swayed toward us, lower, lower, till the vessel was on her beam end. She lay there a few seconds and then disappeared. A cry of horror arose from the lookers on; and, as if by instinct, our ship's head was at once turned towards the scene and the sole survivors of the pretty little schooner. As soon as the poor fellows were able, they told us the story, stating that their vessel was submerged by a gigantic squid, the animal which, in smaller form, attracts so much attention in the Brighton (England) Aquarium as the octopus."

A year later, there was another giant squid attack off Connemara, Ireland. Three men in an open boat came upon an object in the water, which looked like a "floating mass of seaweed." The object then embraced the boat in its arms. The crew, with only one knife among them, managed to chop off its limbs and finally its head. "The rest of the body sank at once," they reported. The battle with the squid lasted over two hours. Upon returning to shore, they showed the squid limbs to Sergeant Thomas O'Connor of the Royal Irish Constabulary; he, in turn, presented the captured arms and head to the Dublin Museum, where they remain preserved today. One of the tentacles on display measures 8 feet, and a second measures thirty feet.

On November 30, 1835, the steamship ALECTON was cruising off the Canary Island when a giant squid surfaced in her path. A battle ensued, and crewmen harpooned the creature. It tried to capture them with its "ten" tentacles, but, within an hour, the crew managed to lasso the squid's tail. The tail was brought aboard, but the rope had cut the creature in half — the head and tentacles sinking back into the depths. After weighing the tial, the crew estimated the squid's weight to be approximately 4,000 pounds, and its length, 60 feet.

Many giant squid and octopus have been captured whole, such as the octopus cast ashore in Denmark after a storm, in 1854. Its body measured 21 feet across; its total length from arm tip to arm tip was 50 feet; and its longest tentacle was 18 feet. In that same year, one was found dead on a beach at Jutland, England, and had twenty-foot arms and a beak measuring nine inches. The largest squid ever captured was found stranded in the shallows off Newfoundland in November 1875. It was dragged ashore by fishermen, tied to a tree, and, when it died a few hours later, was measured. Its arms were 35 feet long, and overall length was 55 feet. Although local dogs ate most of the creature before scientists arrived on the scene, a life-sized replica of this monster is now on exhibit at the Smithsonian Institution in Washington, D.C.

Four fishermen entangled a giant squid in their nets off Logy Bay, Newfoundland, in 1873. The frightened fishermen stabbed at the creature and managed to bring it ashore. A local naturalist, Reverend Moses Harvey, bought the remains of the squid from the fishermen for $10.00. He, and a few others, dragged it to his home where he attempted to preserve it in an outhouse bath. Harvey astounded the scientific world when he reported that the beast was 32 feet long — prior to this, most scientists and naturalists did not believe the stories about giant squid.

Giant squid are often found in the bellies of captured whales. A whale harpooned off Maderia, in 1952, contained a live squid 34 feet long, weighing over 350 pounds. On July 8, 1875, the captain and crew of the ship PAULINE had the rare experience of witnessing a battle between a whale and a giant squid. The captain, George Drevar, and five crewmen describe the encounter as follows:

> "We the undersigned observed three large sperm whales, and one was gripped round the body with two turns of what appeared to be a huge serpent. The head and tail appeared to have a length beyond the coils of about 30 feet, and its girth eight or nine feet. The serpent whirled its victim round and round for about 15 minutes, and then suddenly dragged the whale to the bottom, head first. . ."

It has been concluded that the "serpent" Captain Drevar described was actually a giant squid, since the sperm whale and the squid have been arch enemies, probably since primeval days. Although we know that whales eat squids, scientists are still not certain which giant beast is the predator. It could be assumed that since squids attack boats, which from beneath the surface appear to look like whales, giant squids are possibly the aggressors.

Most marine biologists have concluded that the home and the breeding ground for these monsters is off the coast of Newfoundland, Nova Scotia, and possible Maine. Since the movie "Jaws" was filmed at Martha's Vineyard, off the Massachusetts' South Shore, there seems to be fewer swimmers and bathers in the water; but, certainly, since the real giant squid monster appeared on the Commonwealth's North Shore in 1980, there seems to be fewer people in the water along that shore as well, especially at Plum Island.

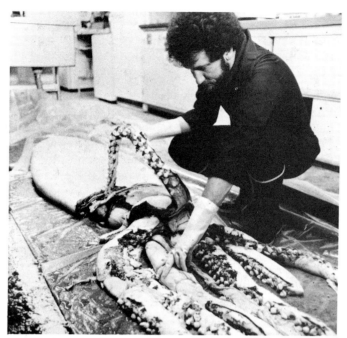

Marine scientist examines the 450 pound, twelve-foot long squid with 16-foot tentacles, that washed ashore at Plum Island, Massachusetts in 1980. Photo courtesy, New England Aquarium, Boston.

The Brig DAPHNE encounters "Nellie" off Boston, on September 20, 1848, and she quickly swims away as the crew fires their deck-guns at her.

II
THE TERRIBLE TRIO — NELLIE, NESSIE, & CHAMP

Most people do not believe in Sea Monsters, or more specifically, sea serpents, and reported sightings of these strange creatures are said to be either figments of warped imaginations or outright lies. History reveals, however, that since the turn of the 15th century there has been at least one sea serpent sighting every year somewhere in the World. On April 10, 1977, what all monster fanatics had been waiting for, happened! A sea serpent was hauled up in the nets of a Japanese fishing trawler, off New Zealand. The 32-foot snake-like creature, with four giant flippers and a long neck and tail, was brought aboard the 2460-ton ship ZUIYUO MARU, from a depth of 1000 feet; but within minutes it was deposited back into the sea. The reason for letting it go, explained Michihiko Yano, a fishing company executive, who was aboard, was because "It was dead and decomposing, and its stench was overpowering. Also, a fatty liquid oozed from the creature, splattering the deck, and we feared it would spoil our cargo of fish." Yano made sketches of the creature, and photos of it were taken, then it was dropped back overboard. In Tokyo, Paleontologists were enraged at the fishermen, believing that they should have at least preserved the skeleton. Professor Yoshinori Imaizumi, Director of Research at Japan's National Science Museum, studied to photos and sketches and determined that the dead monster was a reptile, not a fish or mammal, "and it looks very much like a Plesiosarus, which supposedly became extinct 100 million years ago."

One recorded sighting of a serpent in the sea was on May 12, 1964, when three Norwegian fishermen spotted a 60-foot "sea snake" of Nantucket Island, Massachusetts. Alf Wilhelmsen was first to sight the strange creature swimming only a few hundred feet from his 80-foot fishing vessel, the BLUE SEA. Alf called to his brother Jens and his partner Bjarne Houghan, who were below deck. "At first I thought it was a whale," said Houghan, "but then I saw that its head had humps on it." They described the creature as having a large head, shaped like an alligator's, a tail much like a lobster's, and a spout like a whale's. Its body was round and firm with a series of humps, and it was colored black with white spots. The three men watched it frolic in the water for over thirty minutes. "At one point, it came toward us," said Houghan, "swung along and then moved parallel to us. It left a wake in the stern, like a propeller, and blew air out of the hole in its head. Then it turned its head north and swam away."

This 32-foot sea serpent with four giant flippers, was caught up in the fish net of a Japanese trawler, on April 10, 1977. It resembles a Plesiosarus, thought to be extinct 100 million years ago, and may be the cause of the many sea serpent sightings off Massachusetts and in Vermont. After taking this photo, the fishermen dropped the creature back into the sea because it was decomposing and the stench was too much for them. A.P. Photo.

The BLUE SEA quickly sailed to New Bedford, and the fishermen reported their sighting to the U.S. Bereau of Commercial Fisheries. The next day, Coast Guard and fishing boats went looking for the sea monster. Three days later it was spotted again by the crew of the dragger FRIENDSHIP, about ten miles from where the Norwegians had seen her, 50 miles southeast of Round Shoals buoy. Crewman Thomas Keeping reported, "we circled the monster twice to get a good look at it. We had it in sight for twenty minutes." The Captain of the FRIEND-SHIP, Albert Pike, described the monster's physical makeup exactly as Bjarne Houghan of the BLUE SEA had, adding that, "the creature had barnacles on its sides." Another crewman, John Samagi said, "it was traveling at five knots, and it never sounded once in twenty minutes. Its tail was vertical, not horizontal like a whale's."

In late August of 1962, a group of sports fishermen sighted a similar creature off Cape Cod. Ten men reported that they watched a monster for many minutes, as it swam along the surface "spraying water from a huge barrel-like mouth." In 1957, again off Cape Cod, near Nantucket Island, the six-man crew of the scalloper NOREEN saw a great unknown monster pop to the surface from a depth of 240 feet. The log of the NOREEN tells the story in this way:

"He had a large body and a small alligator-like head. The neck seemed to be of medium size, matching the size of the head. The body was shaped somewhat like a seal. . .He would glide out of the water with the lower part of his body remaining submerged. The portion of his body which was visible measured about 40 feet in length. We estimated his weight to be between thirty-five and forty tons overall. At no time did the whole body show. He stayed on the surface no longer than forty seconds at a time. You could hear the heavy weight of his upper body when he dove below, creating a large splash and a subsequent wake. He surfaced four times in twenty minutes, during which time we were trying to stay clear of him. When the captain changed course to steer away from him, the formidable thing actually appeared to follow the ship. At that point, the skipper ordered the scallop drags to be brought in. When the drags were on deck, he ordered full speed to the westward, away from the sea serpent."

Although the above descriptions fit no known marine animal, the real skeptic might say that in all cases, these men witnessed a whaleshark feeding on the surface. The whaleshark, biggest fish in the sea, can measure 40 feet in length and weigh several tons. It is sometimes colored black with white spots; has wrinkles, or little "humps" on its back near the head; a vertical tail; and has been known to stand upright in the water. In fact, one of its customary habits is to find a school of tuna that are feeding, stand upright in their midst and suck in all the minute morsels that the tuna leave behind. From the surface, the whaleshark's mouth, which is somewhat pointed, might look like a "huge barrel-like mouth spraying water," as one of the Cape Cod monsters was described. On November 18, 1970, a "monster" was found on the beach at Provincetown, Cape Cod, but was later identified as a decaying basking shark. This would not be the first time that a known fish was mistaken for a sea monster.

"Mola Mola" is the name of a known sea monster still greatly feared by the natives of the South Pacific Islands. Mola molas live in deep water and are sometimes seen on the surface off the New England Coast. When they do appear, the sight is appalling, to say the least. A full grown mola mola, better known as a sun-fish weighs 1,200 pounds and is about nine feet long. It has been known to attack boats, but only when molested. Like other monsters, the sun-fish is an even-tempered creature, but, like all other creatures of this world, if wounded or frightened, it may attack. An interesting note about the sun-fish is that at birth it is one-tenth of an inch long. Its size increases over 1,000 times before reaching maturity — and its weight, over 60 million times.

The sea serpent is the most controversial monster in the world. Some people believe that serpent reports are actually the sightings of giant squid tentacles. Tentacles skimming along the surface waters could be mistaken for a giant sea serpent, however, the majority of serpent reports refute this notion. Nevertheless, there have been revealed hoaxes and false sightings concerning sea serpents which please the disbelievers, and make the believers feel a bit foolish. For example: Albert Koch exhibited a 114-foot long skeleton of a sea serpent in New York, in 1845. Thousands came to view in awe the remains of the great monster, and Albert charged them all a good price to see it. Later, it was revealed that Koch had pieced several fossils together to create his sea serpent.

For some unknown reason, most sea serpent reports come from the Atlantic Ocean where there have been sightings almost every year since the days of Columbus. In fact, Columbus himself spotted one during his long journey to the New World. He and his crew caught sight of the serpent while they floated becalmed in the Sargasso Sea. Eight years later, Olaus Magnus, a Swedish archbishop, wrote a history of the Scandinavian nations in which he mentioned the "Kraken," — a great serpent that engulfed ships with its tentacles. Descriptions of the creature Olaus gives in his writings indicate that the "Kraken," as he calls it, was most likely, a giant squid.

During the 18th and 19th centuries, most people, for fear of being ostracized, were reluctant to report their sightings of serpents in the sea. In the summer of 1746, a Norwegian fishing boat sliced into a strange monster floating on the surface. Wounded, the beast sank into the depths, but the captain and crew got a good look at her before she did. The commander of the fishing boat, Lorenz Von Ferry, described the cretaure as "serpent-like, grey, and having a large mouth. It had black eyes, a white mane, and was 70 feet long." The commander reported the accident, but Von Ferry and his crew were so ridiculed and their story so widely disbelieved, that they were taken to a court of law. Von Ferry and three of his crew members swore, under oath, that they had seen and wounded this weird looking creature.

In 1848, the British warship, H.M.S. DAEDALUS, cruising in the Atlantic a few hundred miles south of St. Helena Island, crossed paths with a serpent on the afternoon of August 6. Two officers aboard the DAEDALUS, Lieutenants Sartoris and Drummond, first spied the 90-foot creature swimming by the ship. They called to the skipper, Captain Peter M'Quhae and four of the crew members, who watched the serpent for over twenty minutes.

Captain M'Quhae did not enter the sighting in the log, nor did he mention the sea serpent to anyone when the DAEDALUS docked at Plymouth. M'Quhae was a respected officer of the British Royal Navy and he wanted to remain so. One of the crew members, however, let the story seep out to the TIMES of London. The British Admiralty then demanded that Captain M'Quhae submit a report on the sighting — a portion of which follows:

"It was an enormous serpent, with head and shoulders kept about four feet constantly above the surface of the sea. . .It passed rapidly, but, so close under our lee quarter that, had it been a man of my acquaintance, I should easily have recognized his features with the naked eye; and it did not, either in approaching the ship, or after it had passed our wake, deviate in the slightest degree from its course to the southwest, which it held on at a pace of from 12 to 15 miles per hour, apparently on some determined purpose. The head, that of a snake. . .was never once below the surfce of the water; its color, a dark brown, with yellowish white about the throat. It had no fins, but something like the mane of a horse, or rather a bunch of seaweed, washed about its back."

As he had suspected, the captain became a victim of the usual skepticism. Professors and scientists suggested that the beast was a large seal, or a deformed whale. In a spirited reply to these suggestions, Captain M'Quhae published a second statement in the London TIMES in which he pronounced that the thing he saw "was not a seal, sea elephant, whale, or large shark, but was, in fact, a sea serpent."

Probably the most popular sea serpent, and the one seen by more people than any other, was the 80-foot snake-like creature that went frolicking off the north coast of Massachusetts, in the summers of 1815 through 1820 and again in 1823, 1826, 1833, 1849, 1875, 1877, and 1886. Over 500 people testified to seeing the serpent week after week, first off Gloucester — then off Lynn, Swampscott, Salem, and Nahant, along the Massachusetts north shore, and off the coast of Maine.

Almost everyone who reported the monster to the New England Linnean Society, which later published the accounts, agreed to its length — give or take a few feet; its color — a dark brown; and its caterpillar-like movement. Amos Story of Cape Ann was first to observe the serpent from shore, swimming about one hundred yards from where he was standing. "I have often seen many whales at sea," said Mr. Story, "but this animal was much swifter than any whale. He had the head like a serpent, rather larger than his body. . ." Another resident of Gloucester, Soloman Allen, had this to say, "His head formed something like the head of a rattlesnake, but nearly as large as the head of a horse. . ."

Thomas Perkins, who founded Perkins Institute of the Blind in Boston, also sighted the serpent off Gloucester. "The object moved with rapid motion up the harbor on the western shore. As it approached us, it was easy to see that its motion was not that of a common snake. . .but evidently the vertical movement of the caterpillar. . .I had a fine glass, and was within one-third to half a mile to it. The head was flat in the water and the animal was, as far as I could distinguish, of a chocolate color. I was struck with an appearance in the front part of the head, like a single horn, about nine inches to a foot in length, and of the form of a marling-spike. There were a great many people collected by this time, many of whom had before seen the same object and the same appearance. From the time I first saw it, until it passed by the place where I stood, and soon after disappeared, was not more than fifteen minutes. I left the place fully satisfied that the reports in circulation, although differing in details, were essentially correct." A skipper of one of the Gloucester ships, Captain Tappan, also saw a thing like a horn protruding from the monster's head. A Mr. Mansfield and his wife, respected citizens of Gloucester, said that while taking a drive by the beach near the harbor, they saw the serpent stretched out in shallow water with its tail on the white sand and its head in deeper water.

In 1819, at Lynn Beach, the serpent appeared again. Samuel Cabot, ancestor of Henry Cabot Lodge, wrote: "My attention was suddenly arrested by an object emerging from the water, which gave to my mind the idea of a horse's head...I perceived, at a short interval, three or four more...He moved rapidly, causing a white foam under the chin, and a long wake...At this time he must have been seen by two or three hundred persons on the beach..." An old fisherman of Swampscott, who saw the creature from Nahant Beach, described the experience as follows: "Some two-hundred yards offshore, there was a fish the form of a serpent. It was 80 feet long at least and it swam off towards King Beach. I saw the entire body. It would rise in the water with an undulating motion, then all would sink except the head. I have constantly engaged in fishing since my youth, but never saw anything like this before." A few weeks later, the Reverend Cheever Felch, along with fourteen others, saw the serpent near Manchester, Massachusetts, from the deck of the U.S.S. INDEPENDENCE. Days later, the Reverend was aboard a schooner with a group of men who were ridiculing him about seeing a serpent. The loudest skeptic was the commander of the schooner, William Malbone. As the schooner passed near Lynn Beach, the helmsman shouted, "There's your sea serpent!" The men aboard laughed; but it was no joke. The monster rose out of the water about twenty yards from the schooner. Reverend Felch stated, "His color is dark brown, with white under the throat. That there is an aquatic animal in the form of a snake, is not to be doubted. No man could now convince Mr. Malbone that there is not such a being."

Nathan Chase of Lynn also saw the creature, twice in one day in August of 1819. "The water was smooth and the creature seemed about a quarter mile away; consequently, we could see him distinctly and the motion of his body. Later that day I saw him again off Red Rock. He then passed along about one hundred feet from where I stood, with his head two feet out of water. His speed was about that of an ordinary steamer...I have no doubt that the uncommon, strange rover, which has been seen by hundreds of men and boys, is a form of snake..." Three years later, the British ship LADY COMBERMERE encountered a serpent in the Atlantic, similar in size and description to the one seen off Massachusetts.

Granville Putnam, in 1888, in his writing of the "History of Rockport" (a town near Gloucester, Massachusetts), said: "It has been my belief for some years, that there is some fitful, gigantic wonderer inhabiting our ocean. . .On the afternoon of August 12, I heard the voice of Calvin Pool, Town Clerk of Rockport, at the door of my cottage at Pigeon Cove, saying, 'there is some strange thing in the water; I think it's a sea serpent!' I quickly took my station upon the rail of my piazza, so that my marine glass was about 50 feet above the water and but 36 feet from the shore. The creature was advancing in a northerly direction and but little more than an eighth of a mile from me. I watched it most attentively for about ten minutes — I estimated the length to have been not less than 80 feet — and the head, about the size of a nail cask, while the middle of the body was larger than that of a large man. The color was a dark brown, and it appeared to be somewhat mottled with a lighter shade — none of the 40 or more persons who saw it detected anything that looked like a fin or flipper. Its movement was not that of a land serpent, but of a vertical one — from my elevated position, I could plainly see the movements of the body. . .Its course was direct, its speed uniform, at not more than five miles an hour."

The Massachusetts sea monster, or, most probably, one of its ancestors, was first sighted off Gloucester in 1638, "quiled up on a rock at Cape Ann," so reported John Josselyn, one of Salem's original Puritan settlers. It was spotted from their boat, by Josselyn and his fishing crew. "One man in the boat started to fire at it, but an Indian aboard stopped him, saying that to kill the serpent would bring bad luck." In 1817, a man from a whaling ship, searching for the monster, actually fired at the creature from close range with a ducking gun. The shot penetrated the serpent's head, causing it merely to shake its head and dive underwater. As reported earlier, the monster was again seen numerous times between the years 1817 and 1819.

The most recent reported sighting of "Nellie" as the North Shore monster is now called — was in May of 1975, when skipper John Randazza and his crew, aboard the DEBBIE ROSE out of Gloucester, spotted her while fishing 15 miles off the coast. At first, they observed her swimming in the distance at Middle Bank, off and on for two weeks. One day, she surfaced near the DEBBIE ROSE. "It was swimming away from the boat," reported Randazza, "and we followed it," but the smooth black-skinned serpent, estimated as 70-feet long, "turned and headed right for us." Its head was like a horse's head, with a white ring around it. "My father, whose been fishing out here for over fifty years, shouted to me to 'get the boat out of here', which I did; for we were all scared." "Where could such a monster come from?" Randazza's father asked.

The Sargasso Sea, where Columbus and his crew encountered a sea serpent, is a tract of the Atlantic Ocean stretching north and east of the West Indies to the Azores. It is made up chiefly of floating algae or weed called sargassum. This floating mass of seaweed covers not only an area larger than the United States, but it also blankets one of the deepest areas in the Atlantic Ocean. Its third claim to fame is an abundance of eels. During their twilight years, eels, like salmon, make long migratory journeys. However, eels reverse the procedure by traveling from inland rivers and lakes to the ocean, where they breed and die. Two species of eels, one from Europe and one from America, migrate to the Sargasso Sea for this once in a lifetime spawn. The young ones then leave the Sargasso and, following the Gulf Stream, make their way to the respective continents. It takes the U. S. eels one year to make the trip; whereas the European eels must travel for three years, to return to the homes of their parents in the lakes and rivers of Europe. To reach lakes and ponds located a mile or more from any other body of water, the female eel will move on land at night, breathing air through her skin. Some of these eels have been trapped in fishing nets. The largest known eel to be captured in Massachusetts waters was one weighing 80-pounds and measuring seven feet in length.

A fight to the death between a large conger eel, weighing an estimated 60 pounds, and a seal was witnessed by fisherman Bruce McMillen of North Wales in the Menai Straighs.

"I was about to pack up my tackle," reported Mr. McMillen in 1964, "when suddenly I was aware of a tremendous disturbance on the surface of the water. A seal's head appeared above water and, caught partially in its mouth — thrashing madly, was one of the largest conger eels I have ever seen. The seal appeared to have it firmly gripped behind the head. There ensued one of the most dramatic sea spectacles you could ever expect to observe, causing both contestants to frequently disappear below the surface. The outcome, as far as I could see, was victory for the seal. Truly a battle of the giants, but one in which, I think, the seal maintained the advantage, once he had secured a firm hold on the conger — enormous though it was."

Recently American Scientist Dr. Robert Menzies discovered what, he considers, may be a baby sea serpent. Menzies, aboard his research vessel "ANTON BRUUM", dragged up — from the deep ocean bottom of Peru — a 12-inch long leptocephalus (baby eel). Alec

Ibanez, Dr. Menzies' assistant, said: "It is conceivable that if the leptocephalus has the same growth rate as European eels, it could attain a length of 100-feet — adult leptocephalus could be responsible for age old sailors' stories of huge, wriggly monsters in the vastness of the earth's oceans."

Doctor Anton F. Bruun, of the University of Copenhagen, once discovered an eel larva in the Sargasso Sea measuring over six feet in length. If this larval form had grown to maturity, it would have developed into a snake-like creature over 90-feet long and weighing several tons. Could it be that sea serpents are actually giant eels born and bred in the Sargasso Sea?

Other eyewitness sea serpent reports are exact descriptions of supposed long extinct dinosaurs. For example, those who say they have seen "Nessie," Scotland's famed Loch Ness Monster, report her as being 40 feet long, with a snake-like head and a long tail. This description fits the "elasmosaurus," a large dinosaur of the plesiosaurus family. Although Loch Ness is land-locked, legend has it that Nessie slipped into the Loch as a youth, hiding under the hull of a ship that was transported from salt to the fresh water of the Loch. Many Scotsmen swear that they have seen Nessie bathing on the surface, but some of these stories have been told with tongue-in-cheek. "She always comes out during the tourist season," one old Scotsman was heard to say; but others, mostly those living near the Loch, will swear that they have seen the serpent.

There have been expeditions to the Loch from England, France, and America, all hoping to prove or disprove Nessie's existence. One of the most recent expeditions was sponsored by David James, a Conservative member of British Parliament. He contends, "that a species of monsters, maybe more than one, live in Loch Ness." Nessie was spotted by a tourist in 1933, and since then has been seen at various times by over 200 people. There is record of a missionary, Saint Columba, visiting the barbaric highlands in 565 A.D., who said that he saw "a very large water animal."

In 1951, a foggy, somewhat unclear photo was taken of Nessie by John Stuart of the Scottish Forestry Commission. Again in 1955, a Mr. P. MacNab took a photograph of the monster swimming near the Castle of Urquhart. "I saw something big, undulating, and moving at from eight to 12 knots," said Mr. MacNab, "and I snapped just as the creature was sounding." Another underwater photograph, taken, in 1975 by lowering a camera on a cable into the Loch, shows a portion of an enormous black flipper. The nearest photo of Nessie was taken by Mr. Surgeon in 1934, with a telephoto lens, at a distance of 300 yards; but, of course, many have debated its authenticity. Even movies have been taken of "something big" swimming along the surface of Loch Ness.

Except for a few hoaxes at Loch Ness, an occasional sighting, and the summer rush of tourists to buy plastic serpent replicas at Inveress Shops, Nessie didn't really raise her ugly head again until 1976. That year, two New England research teams rivaled each other for publicity about their various discoveries and authentications of Nessie's existence. Dr. Robert Ballard, a geologist from Woods Hole, Massachusetts led a National Geographic Society team that scoured the lake for two and one-half months. They sent divers down into the murky water, dropped lines of dead fish leading to underwater cameras, used sound signals, and poured sheep's blood on the surface waters, until Loch Ness "looked like an Italian delicatessen," said Ballard. Everything but the monster triggered their underwater cameras; small fish, eels, and even seaweed. Ballard's team discovered that the lake bottom has a great residue of coal, apparently dropped overboard from steamers or from sunken coal barges, and a lot of teapots. "There seems to be more teapots in Loch Ness than anything else," concluded Dr. Ballard.

The second monster hunting team, led by Dr. Robert Rines, president of the Academy of Applied Science in Boston, and sponsored by the New York Times, was more successful than the geographic group; but they, too, were disappointed at not seeing Nessie. The did, however, get a sonar sighting of what might be the carcass of a plesiosaurus-like creature on the Loch bottom. The side-scan sonar device produced a fuzzy outline of an object resembling the prehistoric dinosaur lying on the bottom of Loch Ness. Martin Klein of Salem, New Hampshire, a sonar expert, said the graph produced: "an unusual shape with a long neck-like projection and what possibly could be flippers." "The object was 30 feet long, at a depth of 150 feet." Dr. George Zug, curator of reptiles and amphibians at the Smithsonian Institution, Washington D.C., said the sonar reading "has dispelled my doubts. I am now convinced that a group of large aquatic animals exist in the murky depths of the Scottish Lake."

Monster mania has recently had an upsurge in Vermont's Lake Champlain, as well. It is another case of a monster being around for a long time, and this one, called "Champ," closely fits the description of Nessie and the Massachusetts Serpent. It was first reported almost 375 years ago by renowned explorer Samuel de Champlain, after whom the

118-mile long waterway was named. He said, "it is a great long monster, lying in the lake, allowing birds to land on its beak, then snapping them in whole." The Indians, living in what is now upstate New York and Vermont, in the late 1500's and early 1600's, made sacrifices to a huge green-skinned sea dragon, who, they say, overturned their canoes and ate the occupants. Supposedly it roamed the surface of the lake only at night, but not in the winter, when the lake usually freezes over. In 1981, "Champ," like Nessie, was declared an endangered species, and at Port Henry, New York, there is a law, "forbidding anyone from doing anything to harm, harass, or destroy the Lake Champlain monster." Scuba divers Morris Lucia and Fred Shanafelt think the law should protect Champ's prey rather than the monster itself. They were searching for an old cabin cruiser that had disappeared into Saint Albans Bay, Vermont, when Champ came to call:

"I surfaced about ten feet out from shore," said Shanafelt, looking back to see what had given Morry such a fright. That's when I saw this thing that couldn't have been anything but a sea serpent! It was 40 to 50 feet long, with the head and mane of a horse, and its color was a mushroom gray, and its neck was sticking out of the water about eight feet. As it moved closer to shore, Morry and I rushed to the beach."

"It cocked its head in a child-like manner," Morry Lucia said, "as if it was curious about our appearance, but, although it didn't make any effort to harm us, I wouldn't go back in that water for a million dollars! We watched it for about two minutes. Then, it just sort of turned its head and moved away. After it got a ways out into the water, the head dropped beneath the surface and it was gone."

A few years earlier, Walter Hard, former editor of Vermont Life Magazine, while he and his wife were picnicking at Appletree Point near Burlington, spotted the creature, "and watched it through my field glasses for about ten minutes. The head was large and whitish and round like a beach ball, and my wife thought she saw its body above the water in two or three coils. Hundreds of people saw it, but they have been reluctant to report it."

"I was fishing on the north side of Hero Island with two friends," said Larry Jones of Swanton, Vermont, "when suddenly, there was a tremendous splash about 300 yards from our craft. There was nothing to see at first, only a group of large ripples. Then, out of the depths reared a huge dark form which moved swiftly in a northwesterly direction. Three segments appeared, clearly visible above the water's surface, separated one from the other by about five feet of water, the overall length of the creature being about 25 feet. It moved with incredible swiftness, at about 15 miles per hour, and disappeared in about two minutes."

Some people living along the banks of Lake Champlain are frightened and won't let their children go out in boats; others hunt for Champ; and still others, scoff.

In 1938, a prehistoric fish called a Coelacanth was scooped up alive in a net off the coast of Africa. Prior to this, Scientists believed that the coelacanth was extinct. This prehistoric fish lived with the plesiosaurus and other dinosaurs.

At this moment, there is a terrifying monster on display at the Museum of Comparative Zoology at Harvard University, Cambridge, Massachusetts. It was recently unearthed in North America, and is the skeleton of a reptile which lived in the ocean over 10 million years ago. it is over 40 feet long and has a huge, 10-foot mouth. The teeth of this monster are over one foot in length. Although the number of disbelievers is still in the majority, there seems to be enough evidence to ascertain the existence of sea serpents. Who is to say that such creatures do not exist in the depths today?

According to Joseph Zaryzinski, Vermont Cryptozoologist, "CHAMP," the Lake Champlain Sea Monster, has been spotted many times throughout the summers of 1983 and '84. At South Hero Island, 25 children and 10 adults saw "CHAMP" swim by in July. Young Sandra Manzi snapped this photo of the "water beast." Gamma/Liason Photo.

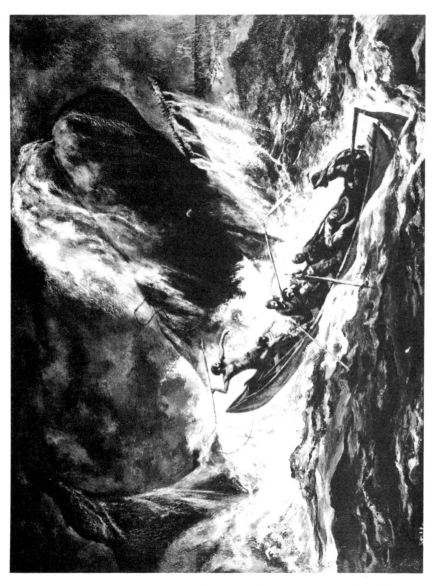

Harpooning the real sperm whale "Mocha Dick", photo courtesy, John Hancock Mutual Life Insurance Co., Boston, MA.

III
A WHALE OF A TALE

The largest animal in the world is the leviathan, or whale, and it is growing larger and larger with the passing of the years. The biggest member of the whale family is the blue whale, which, at maturity, can reach a length of 100 feet and a weight of 300 tons - - in comparison, the largest land animal, the elephant, is about ten feet tall and weighs three tons. Even the size of baby whales is staggering. An unborn whale taken from the belly of a blue whale weighed 16,000 pounds and was 25 feet long. A baby blue whale takes from its mother as much as 200 pounds of milk per day; over a ton of food particles was found in the stomach of a captured adult blue whale.

Whales are air-breathing, warm-blooded mammals, whose ancestors originated on land, roaming the earth some 150 million years ago. Prehistoric whales had legs, and hair all over their bodies, and their jaws contained rows of long, sharp teeth — but these mammals weren't as large as the whales of today. A search for more food caused them to enter the sea, where the abundance of fish increased their size. It was then that their hairy coat disappeared, except for a few hairs that remain around the lips. Even today, the bones in the front flipper of the whale looks like a giant hand, and the hidden bones-far back in the whale's body-resemble hind legs. Today, however, a whale cannot survive out of water for more than a few hours, because when out of water the weight of its huge body presses down on its lungs causing it to suffocate. The whale cannot remain under water for too long either. it must come to the surface every hour or so to exhale through the blowhole on the top of its head, and inhale another breath through the blowhole before it dives again. It is for this reason that whales do not sleep, rather they are forced to take occasional snoozes on the surface. If while snoozing a whale should accidentally turn over on its side, and the blowhole becomes filled with water, the whale drowns.

There are two types of whales, the baleen and the sperm, which together comprise about 30 species, found in all oceans of the World. Baleen whales live on small marine animals such as shrimp. There is not one tooth in their enormous heads. Instead, their palates are furnished with baleen or whalebone, which is used to strain the minute particles on which they feed. The baleen of an average sized whale weighs approximately 800 pounds. The right whale and the Greenland whale — both of the baleen family, sometimes yield up to 3,500 pounds of baleen. Whalers in the 19th century prized baleen when it was used to make women's corsets, buggy whips, and umbrellas.

Sperm whales have jaws up to 25 feet long, with one large row of powerful bottom teeth, but no teeth in their upper jaws. They feed mainly on squid. A male sperm can grow to 65 feet, but the female's maximum length is 40 feet. One of the most famous whales of all times, Moby Dick, was a sperm whale, and although Herman Melville's classic story was a work of fiction, many of the incidents in the book actually happened during the romantic days of Yankee whaling.

At the end of the "Moby Dick" novel, the great white sperm whale attacks and sinks the whaling ship PEQUOD. On November 20, 1820, the ship ESSEX was actually sunk, when attacked by a real sperm whale.

According to seaman Owen Chase - who was aboard the ESSEX when it was whaling in the Pacific off South America, 463 days out of Nantucket - three boats were lowered from the mother ship, early in the morning after spotting a school of sperms. One whale was wounded and managed to escape; it was probably this same 65-foot beast that surfaced, about 30 minutes, later and started swimming at full speed towards the ESSEX. It crashed into the ship just forward of the forechains. The ESSEX started leaking badly. Then the whale appeared again, "about 100 rods to leeward, apparently in convulsions," for it leaped some 20 feet out of the water, snapping its enormous jaw. Then, using its head as a battering ram, it crashed into the ship again, and the 238-ton ESSEX capsized and proceeded to sink. Most of the men, who watched the attack from their 20-foot whaleboats, managed to salvage biscuits and water from the ship before she went under. Then 20 men began their 4,500-mile row to the nearest land. It was 91 days before they were rescued by the British brig INDIAN. Only eight of the 20 ESSEX whalers survived, due only to their reverting to cannibalism during their long open-boat journey.

The KATHLEEN, out of New Bedford, Massachusetts, was also demolished by a great sperm whale in 1902 in the Atlantic. As the ship sank, the entire crew plus a parrot were safely lowered into two boats. It is reported that the parrot was quoted as saying, "I'll be damned if I'll ever go to sea again," and it didn't, for during the nine days at sea, the crew ate it.

In 1851, the New Bedford whaler ALEXANDER, under Captain John Deblois, was rammed by a sperm whale and sank. Her crew was rescued two days later. The whaling ship GRACIA, in 1894, in attempting to take a finback whale was rammed. The ship sank and the crew escaped in longboats. There have also been reports of unintentional collisions with whales that have caused ships to sink or become disabled. The ship UNION hit a whale in the Atlantic in 1807, and just managed to reach the Azores before she sank. Twenty years later, the sloop PEACOCK hit a sperm whale, and was forced into port, leaking badly. On April 29, 1926, the submarine V-1 was badly jarred off Provincetown, Massachusetts; when she came to the surface, there was a 58-foot finback whale draped over her bow. The commander of the sub, Sherwood Picking, towed the whale into Provincetown and offered to sell it for its oil. There were no buyers in the old whaling town, so he towed the whale back out to sea and sank it with a five-inch gun. During World War II, according to Professor E. J. Slijper, "Whales have also rammed, without success, modern metal whaling boats."

The terrible and unusual death of Captain Ahab in "Moby Dick," was nothing new to the whaling world either. A similar fate was actually experienced by Captain C. W. Swain of the whaling ship CHRISTOPHER MITCHELL of Nantucket. As a harpoon was thrust into a whale from the longboat, Swain's leg became tangled in the line, and he was carried into the depths as the whale made its dive. When the whale was later captured, the body of Captain Swain was found lashed to its hide. A seaman of the bark HENRY TABER was luckier than Captain Swain. He managed to climb aboard a whale that had destroyed his longboat with a flick of its powerful tail, and the seaman spent the night holding onto a harpoon that was imbedded deep in the mammal's back. Luckily the whale never sounded, and by morning was floating dead on the surface, with the thankful seaman still clutching the harpoon. The seaman was rescued.

In the novel "Moby Dick," as in the Biblical story of Jonah, whales have been known to swallow men whole. A sperm whale devoured a doctor, who fell over the rail of a British clipper ship, in 1894. A day later, the whale was captured and its stomach removed. the dead doctor was found inside, his body badly mangled, but he was still in one piece.

A more remarkable incident occurred on August 25, 1891, when, early in the morning, the crew of a longboat from the whaler STAR OF THE EAST, out of Britain, harpooned a large sperm whale. The whale, however, turned on the boat, crushing it with its powerful jaw. All the crew but one escaped by jumping overboard. Crewman James Bartley, age thirty-five, was caught in the whale's mouth and swallowed. Later that same day, the whale floated dead to the surface. It was brought along side the STAR OF THE EAST, and for two days, the blubber was hacked from its great body. When its stomach was about to be cut open, the crew saw to their horror, the outline of a human body showing through the membranes. They,carefully sliced through the whale's stomach and there was James Bartley. His flesh was purple and he was smeared with whale blood, but he was still alive. The crew immediately went to work to revive him, and within two hours he regained consciousness. He babbled and screamed and suffered with hallucinations of being burned alive. On the return trip to England aboard the STAR OF THE EAST,he regained his health and senses and reported his bizzare experience:

"When I jumped from the boat, I felt my feet strike some soft substance," he said. "I looked up and saw a big-ribbed canopy of light pink and white descending over me, and the next moment I felt myself drawn downward, feet first, and I realized that I was being swallowed by a whale. I was drawn lower and lower; a wall of flesh surrounded me and hemmed me in on every side, yet the pressure was not painful and the flesh easily gave way like soft India-rubber before my slightest movement. Suddenly, I found myself in a sack much larger than my body, but it was completely dark. I felt about me, and my hand come in contact with several fishes, some of which seemed to be still alive. Soon I felt great pain in my head and my breathing became more and more difficult. At the same time, I felt a terrible heat; it seemed to consume me, growing hotter and hotter. My eyes became coals of fire in my head, and I believed every moment that I was condemned to perish in the belly of a whale. It tormented me beyond all endurance, while at the same time the awful silence of the terrible prison weighed me down. I tried to rise to move my arrms and legs, to cry out. All action was now impossible but my brain seemed abnormally clear; and with a full comprehension of my awful fate, I finally lost all consciousness."

The crew of the STAR OF THE EAST swore to the miraculous adventure of James Bartley under oath, but it wasn't until four years after the incident that newspaper editors dared to publish the story, for they feared public ridicule. Finally, on March 14, 1896, the French journal, Journal des Debats, printed James Bartley's entire story. He lived on for many years to retell his remarkable adventure, but he was scarred for life, for the washings of the whale's gastric juices had partially bleached his skin to a pure white.

Another fascinating story of 19th century whaling was experienced by a Captain Peter Paddock of Nantucket, Massachusetts. On a whaling expedition in 1802, Paddock struck a whale with his harpoon. The harpoon was one he had custom made and his initials were carved into the metal. The whale he wounded this day fought furiously, and managed to escape with the harpoon firmly embedded in its back. Thirteen years later, aboard another whaler, LADY ADAMS of Nantucket, one of Captain Paddock's crew struck and killed a whale and brought it along side the mother ship. Looking down at the blubbery beast from the ship's rail, Captain Paddock couldn't believe his eyes, for there sticking out of the whale's back was his long-lost, rusty harpoon.

Melville's story of a rogue bull sperm whale wasn't so far fetched either, for during the days of Yankee whaling, rogue bulls roamed the sea attacking small whale boats, and living for years with many harpoons in their backs. Old whaling books, written before "Moby Dick" tell of wild bull whales, and how each was given a nickname by local fishermen. There was "Tom" off New Zealand, who Melville mentions in his novel; "Don Miguel" off South America; and one called "Mocha Dick," who traveled the South Pacific. Mocha Dick was a real rogue sperm, according to a journal writtten by J. M. Reynolds in 1839. He was a "whitish" whale that lived for forty years, fighting whalers and attacking boats. "Mocha," says Reynolds, "was blind in one eye and suffered many battle scars, including a twisted jaw." He was finally captured and killed by the crew of the whaling ship PILGRIM off the coast of Chile, sometime between 1810 and 1815. When captured, Mocha Dick had 20 old harpoons in its back. The real life adventures of Mocha Dick influenced Melville to write "Moby Dick."

The 19th Century Yankee whalers preferred the sperm to any other whale; mainly because it contained a greater quantity and better quality of oil than any other species, and because it yielded spermaceti, a spongy odorless substance which was used to make candles. Spermaceti is found in large quantities in the whale's head, and is part of its hydrostatic organ, which helps it to dive and surface. Sperm whales, because of their squid diet, also hold a potential fortune in ambergris. One 34-foot sperm stranded on a beach at Jupiter Island, Florida, in 1965, had 56 squid beaks in its stomach. The amergris, used as a base for perfumes, results from squid beaks being lodged in the whale's digestive tract. The beaks apparently give whales ulcers and the ulcers produce ambergris. Whales also have kidney stones. One stone gotten from a whale is displayed at Mystic Seaport, Connecticut. The stone, 8" by 5", is composed mostly of magnesium.

Ambergris is not only found in a whale's stomach, but often is discovered floating on the surface waters, after a whale has belched it up. The Chinese, as far back as the thirteenth century, prized ambergris, as they did gold and silver. They called it "lung yen" meaning dragor saliva. They used it as a love potion. In India, the spongy substace was supposed to have powers that assisted women in childbirth, and in Persia, it was used in sweets and confections to stir up feelings of love within the populace. When eaten regularly, it was thought to lengthen life. Today, as a base for perfumes, ambergris is still performing seductive duties. Strangely enough, it is not desired because of its sweet odor, but because it has remarkable abilities of maintaining a scent or odor.

The largest mass of ambergris ever found floating on the surface was collected off the Coast of Africa and weighed 900 pounds. The finders received $15 an ounce for it. The largest piece of the valuable gray matter ever found inside a sperm whale, was discovered by the Dutch East India Company off New Zealand in 1880, weighing 982 pounds and worth $125,000. British scientist Robert Clarke found a piece of ambergris inside a 49-foot sperm whale captured in the Antarctic in 1953. The ambergris weighed 926 pounds and measured 5' by 3'. Two Connecticut fishermen literally netted $2,000, when they scooped up 252 pounds of ambergris in Long Island Sound in 1940.

After reading "Moby Dick," one might conclude that oil, spermaceti, and ambergris are the only commercially valuable products to be gotten from whales, when, in fact, every part of the whale, was, and still is, consumed by humans every day: rich whale milk and tasty tongue have been delicacies in some parts of the world since the Middle Ages--a whale's tongue can weigh as much as three tons. Good doughnuts are made from whale blubber and from the whale's pancreas is taken insulin for diabetics. Whale oil, once used for lanterns throughout Europe and America, was also used in face creams, soaps, margarine (50 percent of Europe's margerine was made from whale oil), candles, and as a base for paints and linoleum products. It was also used in the ropemaking, wool, and leather industries. The oil of the blue whale-because it contains glycerine-was used comercially for manufacturing explosives; and sperm oil was highly valued for precision instruments. Whale's teeth are still prized for "Skrimshaw," and sold as necklaces, tie pins, and other personal and home decorations. Whale bone was used for fertilizer, and its innards, for animal feed. Vitamins A and B are extracted from the whale's one-ton liver, and in some countries, its 1/2-ton heart is chopped up for human consumption. Whale meat, which tastes like beef, was consumed in many European countries. The

Japanese eat over 100,000 tons of whale meat annually, averaging about 25 percent of all the meat consumed in Japan per year. The Japanese filet of beef, using whale meat, cannot be equalled anywhere, not even in Texas. Every good-sized whale yields about 40 tons of meat, the same amount a Texas rancher produces out of 130 head of cattle. The tenderloin of a whale is 25-feet thick and about 75-yards long. Because many types of whales are now protected, and its products cannot be exported to certain countries, the consumption of whale meat has declined rapidly in European countries since the mid-1970s.

The captains of Yankee whalers, bringing in as many as 8,100 whales annually, during the 1800's, became rich men. In fact, the whale itself became such an integral part of communities in Nantucket and New Bedford, Massachusetts, that whaling captains offered them as doweries to their marriageable daughters. The young girls of New Bedford, wouldn't think of marrying a man unless he had harpooned a whale. Whaling, however, as illustrated so vividly in "Moby Dick," was not a romantic life. The hardships and tragedies in Melville's classic were real. Usually, 30 men were crowded aboard a whaling ship where food and water were scarce. When whales were caught, blood flooded the deck, and the rancid odor of dead flesh and blubber permeated everything aboard. Wages were not paid to the captain and crews of whaling ships. They received shares in the profits from the whales slaughtered. If no whales were caught, no wages were paid. Some ships cruised the oceans for over a year, returning home without a drop of whale oil. There is one recorded case of a ship returning to port, after three years at sea, without having captured one whale. On the contrary, there was a ship that returned to New England after one year at sea with $300,000 worth of whale oil. America's greatest whale catch was in 1837, when 5,319,138 gallons of oil was brought into New England ports. At that time, there were over 700 whaling ships working out of 34 New England seacoast towns. Whale oil then was selling for 82 cents a gallon. In the 1850's, it sold for $1.60 a gallon.

Another great hardship was the cold and treacherous seas. In 1871, 33 whaling ships were caught and crushed in the ice of the Bering Sea, causing hundreds of men to perish. In 1876, twelve more whaling ships were crushed in Arctic ice flows. The whaler, GREENLAND, cruising the Arctic for whales in 1775, came upon another whaling vessel that was frozen in the ice. Everything aboard the ship was in good order, but the crew were corpses, all victims of exposure. Later, the crew of the GREENLAND discovered, from the log, that this ship had been sealed in the ice for 13 years.

During the Civil War, Confederate raiders prowling the Atlantic, sank many whaling ships and either killed or sent the whalers to Confederate prisons. There was always, of course, the danger of being capsized or killed by the "whack" of a whale's tail, as the whale was being pursued by longboats. When a whale was harpooned, it would often take the flimsy wooden longboat on-what whalers called-"A Nantucket sleigh ride." The wounded whale would either dive or thrash about on the surface, pulling the longboat behind it--and if the boat ventured too close, the large tail would smash down, crushing the boat and crew. Wounded sperm whales have also been known to jump 20 or more feet into the air and land belly down on a longboat. Angry sperm whales have also cut longboats in half with their mammoth jaws, and were known to free other wounded whales by biting off harpoon lines.

Man, however, would usually win his battle with the beast; the spouting of bloody red mist through the whale's blowhole usually signaled the end of the fight. Because of their special blood makeup, which allows them to dive and remain at great depths, whales suffer from hemophilia. Once their flesh has been punctured by a harpoon they often bleed to death.

Yankee whaling died, having prospered for only 34 years, from 1825 to 1859. In that final year, crude oil was discovered in Pennsylvania; this new find initiated the beginning of the end of the Yankee whaling industry. Also, as sperm whales became harder to find-because so many had been slaughtered-whalers pursued the bowhead and its cousin, the right whale. Right whales, growing to a length of 60 feet, are slow swimmers, have no teeth, and, unlike the sperm, float to the surface after death. These qualities make them easier to tow back to the mother ship, however their value is less since their oil is not the high quality found in sperms. Another whale that was hunted throughout the last century and well into the 20th, was the humpback whale, which grows to 50 feet. It is known as a "clown of the sea," because it is often seen frolicking in the water, leaping into the air, twisting and turning, then slamming the surface with its back. Humpbacks have also been seen standing on their heads and beating the surface waters with their flukes. This is thought to be some kind of a mating ritual, performed by male humpbacks to attract the females. Humpbacks also leap into the air and hit the surface waters with a thud in order to rid themselves of parasites and barnacles. One recently captured humpback had 1000 pounds of barnacles growing on its back. As happy-go-lucky as a humpback may seem, it can be mean and irritable, especially in the winter months — no one seems to know why.

A rarity in the annals of sea-lore are stories, some legend, of men riding whales. There's the story of Bernie and Benny Ramsay who spotted a whale entering the river at Chatham, New Brunswick. Bernie fixed a rough-halter to the 18-foot whale and rode it until it swam out to sea. Actually, the whale had been stranded in the shallows and died there before Bernie Ramsay climbed on its back with his halter. Diver Phil Amero of Boston rode a whale into Wellfleet Harbor, CapeCod, back in the 1960's, but the whale was sick and soon died.

Frank Cabral, Jr. and his father were lobstering about half a mile off the shore of Provincetown, Massachusetts, pulling lobster traps from two dories near their 30-foot cabin cruiser. Frank and his dad were about 30 yards apart when a 70-foot finback whale surfaced between them, then submerged again. "It was so close to my father that I saw his dory roll back and forth, from the waves it made," said Frank, Jr.; but he continued pulling traps, "when I noticed the water underneath my dory grow dark, as if a cloud were passing in front of the sun overhead. Then there was a loud crashing of timbers and planks beneath my feet. My boat and I were thrown about ten feet into the air by the violent impact, and I was thrown out of the boat. To my surprise and terror, I didn't land in the water. I landed with a thud and, putting my hands down, I could feel the slick back of the whale moving under me. It was moving forward and I was sliding backward. The few seconds I remained on its back seemed an eternity--the whale finally submerged and I was carried down into the ocean by his trememdous undertow I struggled frantically to overcome the suction, but to no avail..Then I was left behind as the whale swam into the depths. Dark water closed around me, as I was still caught in the suction. My rubber boots filled with water, combined with the weight of my oilcloth, made me feel like I was weighted down with an anchor."

Frank Cabral, Jr. finally struggled to the surface and clung to the wreckage of his dory before his father rescued him. He was out lobstering the following day and, says Frank, "Sure enough there was Willie, the old finback, spouting gleefully to greet us."

Another fisherman, Herman Bendixen of King Cove, Alaska, caught a whale in his crab pot. Captain Bendixen was lifting his pots 20 miles off Cape Lutke, when "one king crab pot came up harder than the others," and no wonder! When he got the 7-foot by 7-foot pot to the surface, a 20-foot finback whale was jammed halfway through it. The whale was dead and Bendixen and his crew towed it ashore. The Captain is quite proud, however, for he is the first and probably the last to ever catch a whale in a crab pot.

Divers Hans Hass and Stan Waterman were recently given the breathtaking mission of swimming alone with a school of whales, in the Atlantic, to take photos of the giant mammals and to record any sounds they made underwater. At a lecture in Boston in 1980, Mr. Waterman expressed his feelings about swimming with whales.

"Being there in the darkness of the depths with hundreds of whales swimming around me was the most eerie feeling I shall ever experience. However, one soothing thought, while down there, was that whales haven't attempted to swallow human beings in a long time."

Another whale issue which caused a lot of hot and heavy debate, in the winter of 1966, was when the Canadian government put an 80-ton, 60-foot finback whale on relief and allocated $1,000 for its care and feeding. Some taxpayers were upset about giving welfare to a whale, but, for the most part, the people of the Newfoundland fishing village of Burgeo were happy with Premier Joseph Smallwood's decision. Burgeo villagers appealed to the Legislature for the financial support of their whale "Moby Joe." Moby, while chasing herring, leaped over a submerged reef and landed in a saltwater pond at Burgeo. It was trapped in the pond which is only 300 yards long and 50 feet deep. Moby tried to escape by swimming back over the reef, but failed at every attempt. He would have to wait for Spring, when high tides would allow escape. Some people tried to kill Moby Joe by blasting at him with rifles and shotguns, but the Premier then warned that, "anymore attacks on government property would lead to prosecution of offenders." Some boys tried to frighten the whale by speeding around it in motorboats, but the villagers stopped these antics. So, for three months, Moby Joe was fed herring with government funds until the flood tides came and he was able to slip away to sea, thanking the good people of Burgeo with a flip of his tail.

Today, the whaling industry is bigger than ever. Automatic guns have replaced the harpoons, and 15,000-ton ships, each with a crew of over 400 men, have taken over the high seas in a quest for whales. These modern factory ships are equipped with radar, spotter airplanes, metal catcher vessels, gymnasiums, barbershops, movie theaters and all other necessary equipment and extra conveniences available. These ships have the capability of converting twelve 120-ton whales into various consumer products within 24 hours. One of their main sources of supply is the finback whale, which is one of the fastest swimming and most powerful of the whale family.

From 1900 to 1980, whalers slaughtered eight times the number of whales that had been killed by the swashbuckling 19th Century New England whalers. Yet, today, these modern whaling methods produce only one-half the amount of oil brought ashore 50 to 100 years ago. The procedures are better, but the whale supply is slowly-but-surely diminishing. It is said that some whales live to be 100 years old, but now that big whales are gone, today's whalers are killing off the smaller whales which contain less oil. Even though America and 13 other countries have outlawed whaling and the import of whale products, the mass slaughter continues. The whale, like the American buffalo, could someday be completely annihilated, and the marvelous leviathan that it took nature 100 million years to create, could someday be destroyed by man.

Scuba diver Phil Amero rides a whale off Wellfleet, Massachusetts.

Lloyd Coffin of Marblehead, MA, displays a 400 lb. Blue Shark caught off Gloucester, photo by Lee Hersey. To the right, the gaping mouth and needle-like teeth of a Goosefish, caught by diver Bill Smith off Beverly, MA, and a rare type of Rock Fish, with several poisonous spines on its back, photo by Paul Tzimoulis.

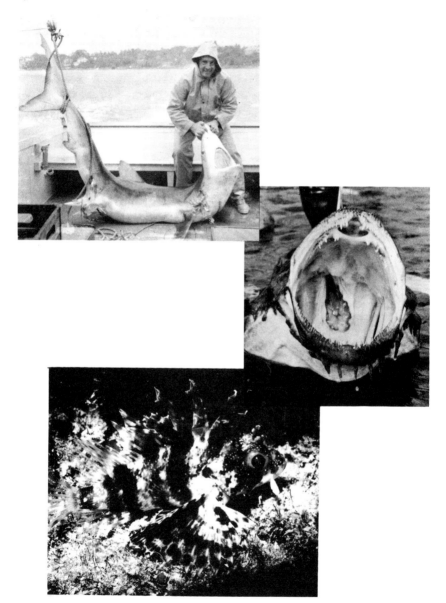

IV
SHARKS AND LITTLE MONSTERS

We were scuba diving off the Isles of Shoals, a cluster of eight small islands about ten miles off Portsmouth, New Hampshire. Gil Arrington and my brother Jim Cahill were first over the side of the 45- foot cabin cruiser, as Ron Carroll and I, on deck, struggled into our rubber suits and scuba gear. Within minutes, Gil was back on the surface, shouting up to us to hand him his speargun. "What do you need a gun for?" I asked. "Sharks down there," he replied matter-of-factly, "hundreds of them," then he disappeard back into the 70-foot depths. I was only 18 years old at the time, and this was to be one of my first dives into, what I considered deep water. This was Ron Carroll's first ocean dive, and he didn't relish the thought of being surrounded by sharks either . . . . We plunged in anyway, and nervously headed for the sea bottom. At about a depth of 50 feet, the kelp strewn rocky floor came into view, and then I spotted Jim and Gil. Circling them were some 60 sharks, not the man-eating variety, but slinky four-foot sand sharks.

One swam over and nipped my fin. Gil pushed it away with the point of his speargun, but he poked too hard. Blood gushed from the shark's belly. The others went after their wounded companion, tearing at it with their sharp teeth. That was enough for me - up I went.

Sand sharks, also called dogfish in New England, are not considered dangerous to man, but the spiny sand shark has a stinger at the forward tip of its dorsal fin that contains venom. When injected into humans, this venom can cause death. New England fishermen hate sand sharks more than any other creature in the sea, yet they catch over 27 million of them every year - but not by choice - the sharks simply get tangled in the nets and are hauled aboard. Fishermen have estimated that the annual damage to other fish and fishing gear by sand sharks is upwards of $5 million, over $400,000 in Massachusetts fishing gear alone. When large schools of sand sharks visit the fishing grounds, all other fish disappear. The depletion of haddock off New England has been blamed on sand sharks; some Gloucester fishermen have suggested that the government inoculate sand sharks with a fatal disease, to get rid of them. In Europe, however, the sand shark is sold as food, and the rich fish oil from its liver is also sold commercially. In England, sand sharks are often served in the famous "fish and chips"; and in Japan, sand sharks are made into sausages and peddled at baseball games, eaten in a roll, much like the American hotdog.

From New England to New York, there have been 22 unprovoked shark attacks recorded in the last 125 years,with just nine of these resulting in fatalities - yet four were victims of supposedly harmless sand sharks. The other five were eaten by the notorious great-white shark, popularized in the movie "Jaws", filmed at Martha's Vineyard, Masschusetts. The first recorded fatal shark attack in New England waters, was in 1815, off the coast of Connecticut, by a hammerhead shark.

The hammerhead shark with its T-shaped head, is considered dangerous, but is not often found in our waters. The white, or great white shark,is voracious and will attack bathers and boats without being provoked. It is found in every ocean, but is not common anywhere. Most great white attacks have been off Australia, South Africa, and America's South West Coast. The great white's first cousin, the mackerel shark, or porbeagle, is prevalent off the New England coast. It can grow to 30 feet in length and weigh four tons or more, and like its great white cousin, has six rows of razor sharp teeth.

A friend of mine, Jack McKenney, who recently led a team of divers to explore the sunken ANDREA DORIA, some 60 miles off Nantucket Island,ran into a school of porbeagles and blue sharks on the surface waters over the wreck site.

"We were constantly aware of these sharks sunning themselves on the surface," said McKenney, "and a number of times, while we were working underwater, they would swim in, to within five or six feet of us. One time, I looked back over my shoulder when I felt a tingling sensation in the back of my neck, and there, not three feet away, was a seven foot blue shark making a turn in my direction. It eyed me for a moment then swam away."

One sultry August afternoon in 1982, I was aboard the cabin cruiser OFFISH out of Beverly, Massachusetts, with owner Mike Aulson. We were off Halfway Rock near the mouth of Salem Harbor, when I spotted a giant fin heading straight for the boat. This fin made the dorsal fin of "Jaws", as depicted in the movie, look like a toothpick in comparison. Mike's own jaw dropped as he watched this monster approach us, and remembering how the great white in the movie attacked and demolished a cabin cruiser, he quickly tried to steer the OFFISH out of its path. He was too late. We stared spellbound into the clear water as the giant passed under the boat. From where I was standing, the creature looked like the real Jaws, with a large grey-white head, beady eyes, and a bulky frame, but it was swimming on its side. What we thought was the dorsal fin above the surface waters, was actually one of its pectoral fins. It wasn't as long as a great white shark either, only about 12 feet, but it had to weigh over 1,000 pounds. It was a sunfish, a fish greatly feared by Pacific Island natives, and seen often here, but not feared at all by New Englanders. It can't swallow anything larger than your fist, but it has been known to attack boats by butting them with its head, if provoked. It is not unusual to see sharks in harbors and close to shore when New England waters warm up, usually in August. One entered Manchester Harbor a few years ago, and the Salem Harbor Master was criticized in the local press for shooting at it and trying to kill it. Of course, if the shark had bitten off some bather's leg, everyone would have been out in their boats trying to kill it. I'm sure that if I had been in the water instead of aboard the OFFISH when that sunfish swam by, I would have died of a heart attack before I had even a chance to find out what it was.

Spending many years scuba diving in New England waters, I have met up with some ugly little fish that I consider monsters. There are many kinds of salt water eels that are fished for, usually after the sun goes down, and are tasty eating. The conger is one of these tasty and testy eel. It is feared by scuba divers, mainly because it hides out in caves and under kelp, where they probe for lobsters. It can give a nasty bite with its human-like teeth, used to crush clam, scallop, and lobster shells. Local fishermen will tell you that the conger can easily bite off metal fishing hooks, and often, when they take a bite of something, like a finger, they won't let go. My brother Jim met a 5-footer underwater that frightened him, and that evening he set a meat-baited hook on a buoyline into the eel-grass, where this larger than normal creature was living. Pulling the hook next morning, Jim had his feisty eel, which he hauled onto a Marblehad beach. The eel remained alive for over an hour, squirming when anyone touched it. One young boy stuck a board in its mouth and the eel clamped down on it. I returned to the beach many days later when the conger was almost a skeleton, but I still couldn't pry the board out of its mouth.

Conger eels are usually about a foot long and live all along the New England Coast. The largest ever caught off our Coast was 9 feet long, but in 1778, at Wicklow Bay, England, C. Gould reported that a Major Wolf was chased out of the water by a large eel, "With a huge bulldog head." The conger eel attacked the major, but he was able to fend it off. English writer Gould also mentions that a few years earlier, a Wicklow farmer named Burbridge was attacked by possibly the same large conger in the bay. Burbridge said, "the giant conger was some 20 feet long."

Two 12 years old boys were fishing from a rowboat off the coast of Boston in July, 1943, and saw a goosefish come to the surface and swallow a duck that had been paddling around near their boat. The boys managed to hook the goosefish, and, when they cut it open, found the duck still alive inside. They nursed the duck back to health and kept it for a pet, for the rest of its natural life. The goosefish is one of the ugliest, most repulsive creatures in the sea. A member of the angler family, it has a worm-like appendage dangling from its forehead, which it uses as a lure to catch smaller fish. It usually sits on the bottom, covers its flat body with sand or mud and waits for its unsuspecting victims to swim by. The mouth of the goosefish is almost as big as its body; when a fish snaps at its appendage, the goosefish merely yawns and gobbles it up. It walks along the ocean bottom on ventral fins that look like human hands and pectoral fins that resemble human arms. Occasionally it will swim to the surface to catch a duck or gull. New England divers have reported being chased by goosefish, some of them, they say, measuring up to four feet, which is large for a goosefish. Only twice in my days of diving have I met up with goosefish. Neither time did the fish show aggression, but just that big, half-moon smiling face, sent a chill down my spine, as did the knowledge that behind that smile was a row of needle-like teeth: The Goosefish, however, is good to eat and is sold at city fish markets, under the name, "Monkfish," for over $4.00 a pound.

Ten year old Robert O'Neil of Dorchester, Massachusetts, was playing on Nantasket Beach, near Boston, on July 15, 1952. He started poking at a flat fish he saw lying in the shallow water. The 20-pound goosefish jumped out of the water and swallowed Robert's arm up to the elbow. A lifeguard ran to Robert's aid and forced the fish to let go by continuously hitting it with a shovel. When the goosefish released the boy's arm, it grabbed the shovel, leaving needle-like punctures in the metal. Robert was rushed to the hospital, where he received treatment for 15 deep teeth marks and several lacerations in his arm.

The goosefish, conger eel, and sand shark are little monsters, living off the New England Coast, of which bathers, swimmers, divers and surfers should be wary - but don't let them keep you out of the water. Just keep in mind that, within the last 7 years, although ten people around the world were killed by sea creatures (eight of them by sharks), within that same period, 16 were struck and killed by lightning and 17 died from bumble bee bites.

V
STRANGE CREATURES OF THE ABYSS

When I was a boy, I once asked my father, who was a commercial fisherman and a sailor in both world wars, "what is the most dangerous fish in the underwater world?" His answer was, "the codfish". I had been catching codfish for years off the New England coast and they didn't seem very dangerous to me. The abundance of cod off our shores was, in fact, the main reason, besides religious persecution, that Europeans came to settle America. The "sacred cod" is the emblem of Massachusetts, and not only was the staple of the New England diet, but its export provided the initial wealth for Yankee merchants. How could the codfish be the most dangerous fish in the sea? "In schools," my father explained. "The cod can strip a swimming dog to the bone within seconds, when it's in a feeding frenzy. A school of fish, be they cod, bluefish, cunner, or any other hungry variety, will tear into a wounded or bleeding animal or human, like piranhas and barracudas."

Even the little herring, when in large schools, can frighten off larger fish, including sharks that are intent on eating them. They have a protector called the "King Herring," also known as the "sea-cat". This strange looking, somewhat shark-like fish grows four or five times larger than the herring, but it is allowed to swim with them. The sea-cat has wing-like fins and its eyes shine in the dark; it also has a fleshy knob that looks like a crown located between its eyes. Thomas "Tub" O'Donnell, now in his eighties, of Bath, Maine, recently told me the following story about King Herring.

"I was out in the bay in a rowboat, when I was in my late teens, with a pretty little gal who was a governess for one of the wealthy families; with us, to my dissatisfaction, was the rich little boy, of whom she was in care, and a wonderful Newfoundland dog, belonging to the boy. "I usually like children," said O'Donnell, "but I must say that this boy was a pest. Always into mischief. It took the pretty governess all her time to prevent the little scamp from falling overboard. Finally, after I had rowed a good half mile off shore, he proved too much for her and slipped from her grasp, pitching head first into the sea. Before I could get up from my seat to assist him, the dog jumped in after him. Seizing him by the collar, before he sank, the noble animal bore him to the side of the boat, and I hauled him aboard. I was about to haul the dog up too, when a great fish suddenly flashed through the water at him, and snapped off one of his hind legs. It would have bitten him again, had I not managed to get him on board in time. The fish did not go away until I picked up an oar and struck it several times. It was probably 6 feet in length, and looked more like a sea-cat than anything else. The poor dog recovered, but spent the rest of its life limping. The governess confided in me afterwards that she would far rather the fish had bitten the boy and, upon my word, I couldn't help wishing so, too."

There is another dangerous fish that travels up to New England, following the Gulf Stream in the summer months, traveling in what could be termed schools. It was probably the first swimming creature on earth, and possibly the most dangerous little animal in the sea. We call it the jellyfish. In Australia, a jellyfish called the "sea wasp" has caused more deaths than sharks. The tentacles of some jellyfish can extend 25 feet from the inverted bowl-like body. In these stinging tentacles are powerful toxins that can paralyze and kill humans. Jellyfish sometimes use these tentacles to wrap around their victims, but most often they puncture their prey with stingers. Most jellyfish swim on or near the surface waters and often invade beaches. Jellyfish, when in larva form, attach themselves to the ocean bottom; before reaching maturity, their mouths are on top of their bodies rather than underneath, where they are located later in life.

The most dangerous jellyfish is the "Portuguese man-of-war." It has long stinging tentacles that extend to 60 feet from its body, and contain a poison that can terminate human life on contact. The man-of-war is not just one fish but a colony of little animals called "polyps". Together, they look like a fleet of miniature 15th century Portuguese galleons under full sail - thus the name. The Portuguese man-of-war maneuvers like a sailing ship too, with its colorful bladder jutting some six inches above the surface waters to catch the wind, and its long tentacles, that can be lowered or retracted at will, operating as a rudder or sea anchor to prevent it from being beached. Even if a man-of-war is chopped into tiny pieces, each small particle has the ability to sting, or possibly kill. Marine biologist Charles Lane, who first isolated man-of-war toxin and found it a beneficial antibiotic, also discovered that man-of-war venom can penetrate rubber gloves; even when frozen or dried, the tiny particles retain their stinging power.

There are many loners in the sea too - fish that prefer to hunt for food alone - and some, like the stingray, skate, toadfish, rockfish, stonefish and torpedo fish, can give a painful sting from barbs located on their backs, or, in the case of the skate and stingray, from barbs at the base of their tail. All of these stinging fish prefer to sit on a muddy or sandy bottom. Hardly a New England summer goes by that someone wading in shallow water doesn't step on one and suffer the consequences. The stonefish and rockfish resemble the implication of their names, and, although only a few inches long, each can have as many as 13 barbs on its back. Its sting has been compared to that of a cobra snake. The venom attacks the human nervous system; the victims can suffer from continuous fainting spells for months after being stung. The skate, plentiful in New England waters, is often caught and eaten by fishermen - its meat tasting much like scalllops. It will never attack, but if touched, it will attempt to stab with its poisonous barb. The sting can cause paralysis and excruciating pain.

The black sheep of the skate or ray family is the torpedo fish. This two-to-four foot creature does not have a barbed tail. Instead, nature provides it with a series of cells, found in its head, that generates an electric current capable of giving humans a severe shock. About 2,000 years ago, Roman doctors often persuaded their patients who were suffering from gout to stand on torpedo fish, as a cure. The electricity from the fish numbed the patients' feet and legs, thereby alleviating the pain. In New England, in the early 18th century, it cost gout patients two shillings and sixpence to be treated by a "torporific fish."

Eels, octopus, catfish, and lampreys, can actually leave the water and hunt on land for food. Octopus have been seen dragging rats, dogs, and - in Oregon - a woman from the shore clutched in its arms. Catfish have been known to steal chickens from coops along the rivers of South America; Florida officials are still up in the air about what to do with lungfish, cousins of the catfish, that walk in mass from one pond to another, depleting all ponds of eatable fish. In the North, the ugly eel-like lamprey leaves the water and climbs over rocks by using it suckling mouth to move from one place to another. The name lamprey means "rock sucker," and the lamprey's mouth, which never closes, secretes a chemical called "lampetrin" that rots fish flesh on contact. The lamprey attaches its strong mouth to a fish, then its row of jagged teeth-located on the tongue- cuts through into the intestines. Lampreys can live in fresh water as well as salt, and can grow to a length of three feet. They fear nothing and will attack anything, including whales. Their cousin, the slime eel (also called "hagfish") attaches itself to other fish and eats away until the entire fish has been consumed. The hagfish, like the lamprey, goes through life with its mouth open; it also has a toothed tongue. It prefers to hunt in deep water up to 300 feet and, because it is without fins, it moves very slowly in the water. To add to the hagfish's navigational problems, it is totally blind.

Another true monster of the deep found off New England, which, like the hagfish, is fairly rare and prefers deep water to shallow, is the wolf-eel or wolf-fish. These furry looking creatures have fierce, dog-like faces with canine teeth to match -which they will use without hesitation. Marine biologists say, however, the wolf-fish in captivity can become fairly tame. They can grow to eight feet in length, and are thought to be eels, only because of a tapering tail. They prefer cold dark water. The few scuba-divers I know who have met up with wolf-fish, have described the encounters as "nightmarish". My scuba diving nephew Mike Cahill, said,"it was like meeting Frankenstein in my bedroom closet."

North of New England, off Queen Charlotte Islands, Canada, in 1934, a fisherman pulled up a strange creature, only six-inches long, but it had a mouth that was bigger than its body. It had big eyes, and its skin was luminescent. No one had ever seen a fish like this before, and no one saw another one like it until 1972. This time, the ugly little creature was caught by members of the Canadian Fisheries Research Department. The fish was preserved for study. In the laboratory, Canadian biologists determined that, although the fish had large eyes, it was almost totally blind. A retractible rod carried on its forehead, with a light on the tip of it, they decided, was used to lure smaller fish into its huge mouth. It was identified as a member of the "Onierodidae family," and as one of the biologists joked, "it is from one of the deep sea Mafia families, that live at 14,000 feet, and can swallow fish twice its size."

There are some deep water creatures that come to the surface at night looking for food. They follow deep scattering layers of plankton, made up of minute particles of animals and plants, that rise from the deep at night when the upper waters cool. Lantern fish, living at 1,000 to 3,000-foot depths, have been seen in schools on the surface in the Antarctic and some 400 miles off the New England coast. The skipper of the British steamer WEATHER OBSERVER, cruising in the Atlantic, in May, 1982, reported sailing for five hours through, "a sparkling display of lantern fish." The lantern fish is only four to six inches long and looks much like any other fish, but it has flashing light organs growing on its head and body that sparkle in a multitude of bright colors. When a new day dawns, the lantern fish return to their nightmarish world of bitter cold and perpetual darkness..

Marine scientists call this virtually unexplored underwater world, "the abyss." Only within the last fifty years has anyone even attempted to visit it. It is the last and largest of the earth's frontiers, and yet its mysteries have been with us since Adam and Eve. The abyss, from depths of 800 feet to 35,800 feet, is where no sunlight ever penetrates. Here on land, you and I experience a constant 14.7 pounds of pressure per square inch on our bodies, whereas, in the abyss, every creature living there has a constant 7 to 8 tons of pressure per inch pushing on its body. Besides eternal night and crushing pressure, the intense cold immediately saps a person's energy, and, if the cold won't do it, the bone chilling fright of real monsters lurking in the darkness surely will. The abyss is uncharted, untamed, and untouched, yet its 115,000,000 square miles makes up 61% of the Earth's surface. One of the main reasons that the abyss remained virgin territory for so long is that, up until about 100 years ago, most scientists were convinced that where sunlight does not penetrate, no life can exist.

"The popular notion was," wrote British marine scientist Sir Wyville Thomson, in 1872, "that after arriving at a certain depth the conditions become so peculiar as to preclude any other idea than that of a waste land of utter darkness, subjected to such stupendous pressures as to make life of any kind impossible." On May 10, 1876, Wyville Thomson and a few of his inquisitive friends returned to England after a 3½ year oceanographic research voyage around the world, aboard the H.M.S. CHALLENGER. They had gathered marine specimens from depths of up to three miles, and had brought back over 4,700 new species of sea animals which no one had ever seen or heard of before. The CHALLENGER voyage still holds the record as the longest and most successful ocean science expedition in history.

Using a newly invented net-dredge, Thomson and his associates dragged the muddy bottoms of every ocean in the World. "It was a thrill beyond my dreams," he said, "bringing up specimens from the deep, but the greatest thrill was to bring up something alive and moving from such a crushing depth. It was the biggest surprise," said Thomson, "as it rolled out of our dredge and settled quietly on deck. It was the form of a round cake, and it began to pant like a dog.... I had to summon up some resolution before taking the weird little monster in my hand."

The first person to venture into the abyss was American zoologist William Beebe, in 1930. Beebe and Otis Barton invented and built a bathysphere, a spherical steel ball with portholes and external searchlights for observation. Suspended by a cable to a surface ship, the bathysphere was dropped to 1,300 feet, and on a second dive, in 1932, to 3,000 feet. Beebe and Barton reported seeing many new strange creatures, including one that looked somewhat like a barracuda, but it had teeth that glowed and a body that radiated a bluish light. "It was over six feet in length," said the excited Beebe upon his return to the surface, "and, since I was the first person in the world to ever see it, I think I have the right to name it. "He called it, "The Untouchable." He also reported seeing a strange looking shark with pop-eyes; and a twenty-foot creature that did not have eyes or fins, but swam with little effort; schools of brilliantly illuminated lanternfish, with pale green and yellow lights; and "hundreds of shrimp whose bodies flashed like red flash bulbs."

To improve on Beebe's bathysphere, two Swiss scientists, balloonist Auguste Piccard and his son Jacques, invented the bathscaphe. Its advantages were that it didn't need a cable or line to a surface ship; it could be navigated up to a mile in any direction underwater; and it could move up and down at the will and whim of its two pilots inside, hovering at any depth they desired. On February 15, 1954, the bathyscaphe penetrated the abyss to 13,000 feet, and on a subsequent dive to 6,900 feet off Sicily, four French scientists aboard got the thrill of a lifetime. . Spotlights and mackerel baited hooks were attached to the outer hull of the bathyscaphe to attract fish. The wide-eyed scientists peered through the portholes and watched large slant-teyed sharks, never before seen by man, appear on the scene and go into a feeding frenzy. They rocked the bathyscaphe, ripping at the bait with sharp glowing teeth, swallowing the hooks then spitting them out like seeds. The Scientists observed a large ray-like fish with bulging eyes and an antenna-like dorsal fin; a foot-long black sea spider; a plant that walked along the bottom; and a fish with two tails, which used them as legs to hop along the muddy bottom like a cricket. The awe-struck scientists were quick to inform their colleagues that the abyss was not only teeming with life but also inhabited with unique life forms, never before seen or imagined by humans.

Jacques Piccard and U.S. Navy Lieutenant Donald Walsh plunged to a depth of 35,800 feet in the bathyscaphe TRIESTE, on January 23, 1960. They were in the Marianas Trench in the Pacific, the deepest spot on the ocean floor, and at that depth, they spotted a tiny shrimp and a foot-long flounder. Coincidentally, on the very day that TRIESTE was making the world's deepest plunge, Harvard College in Cambridge, Massachusetts, was exhibiting, for the first time, hundreds of living fossils dredged up from the abyss by the Danish research vessel GALATHEA. Highlighted was a large deep sea clam thought to be extinct for 350 million years, and a new type of angler fish-looking somewhat like the goosefish, but with a luminous pendant in its mouth-used to attract other fish, like a candle flame attracts moths. Leader of the Danish expedition, Dr. Anton Bruun, named the foot-long angler fish "Galatheathauma Axeli," after his ship. Considered by many to be the most important catch of the GALATHEA was a great sea-slug. It was hauled up from 23,400 feet, where it spends its entire life trudging slowly through the oozy bottom mud, which it eats to get minute particles of food. In order to avoid suffocation, its tail is a natural periscope used to breathe oxygen from the water above. Its body is shaped like a military tank, with many sets of legs, which it uses to bury itself. The GALATHEA crew brought up another tank-like creature of the sea-cucumber family. It had six sets of legs, and two sets of horns, front and rear, which gives it the appearance of a miniature bull, coming and going. The GALATHEA biologists learned the hard way that the horns were actually quills that contain a potent sting. They also fished up a foot long bristle-footed worm with silky skin; when touched, sharp spines darted out of its skin, producing a long, painful sting - another fact these marine pioneers had to learn the hard way. Today, in handling all creatures from the abyss, marine biologists wear rubber gloves.

Nine years after the TRIESTE deep dive and the Harvard GALATHEA exhibit, Jacques Piccard surfaced from thirty days in the abyss, off the coast of Massachusetts, south of the Grand Banks. He had piloted his bathyscaphe BEN FRANKLIN some 1,500 miles from Palm Beach, Florida, following the Gulf Stream. His "drift" in the abyss was sponsored by the American government. While he and his six-man crew were drifting at depths from 2,000 to 4,500 feet beneath the Atlantic, America's astronauts were making their first landing on the moon. Although many of Piccard's findings during a month stay aboard the 48-foot FRANKLIN are still designated Top Secret, by the U.S. government, it was revealed that he discovered a large swift current running in a southerly direction, opposite to the drift of the Gulf Stream, and moving directly under it. The FRANKLIN also bumped into a mountain peak at 1,800 feet off New Jersey, which, until then, nobody knew was there; they also encountered new life forms. As Piccard commented when he reached Boston, "we learned much during our mission, but most of all we learned how little we know about the abyss."

It was Boston born Ben Franklin who discovered the Gulf Stream, and it was also Ben who, in 1753, suggested that many deep water fish have their own built in electric light system. You have probably never visited the abyss, and neither did Ben Franklin, but he, like yourself, had seen those magical sparks of light on the surface waters at night, called "phorescence." Ben concluded that those lights on disturbed water surfaces were caused by microscopic sea organisms, "the luminescence of living things," he called it. Today, marine biologists call it "biolumines-cence," and they are convinced that the thousands upon thousands of strange creatures that inhabit the abyss, most of which nobody has yet seen, are almost all "bioluminescent" - In other words, they light up the abyss like New York at Midnight.

One of the most common abyss creatures is the five-inch long hatchet fish. Its skin is made up of silvery irredescent pigment, and it has light producing organs imbedded in its skin, as well. The hatchet fish can control these lights to blink on and off through its nervous system. Some hatchet fish twinkle blue while others emit a red glow: why the different colors, as yet no one knows. The ugly little fish is aptly named, for its body is thin and sharp at the edges, shaped like the blade of a hatchet. Its big eyes are always looking upward, which seems to indicated that its food filters down through the waters from above.

The deep sea krill and shrimp, like the ones Beebe saw glowing through his bathysphere window, light up the abyss like fireflies, with little candle-like organs attached to their stomachs that flicker red, purple, green and yellow. There are long-legged crabs that clutter the deep sea bottom: they have big eyes and live in snail-like shells that are covered with luminous anemones. These crabs also have lights on their stomachs to guide them through the darkness. The anemones, called sea-pens and sea-fans, are flowery polyps that give off waves of multicolored flickers, lighting up the sea bottom like campfires in the wilderness. There are plant-like animals, such as sea-lilies and comb-jellies, that sway with the undercurrents, producing waves of colorful lights; the jellyfish, "aequrea", has a body that is made up mostly of luminous protein. Marine biologists believe that the aequrea may be responsible for much of the constant light in the abyss.

There have been two recent monster reports from the abyss. One was from Ron Church, noted scuba diver and now a pilot of the submersible DEEPSTAR 4,000. Ron and co-pilot Wes Andrews were inside DEEPSTAR at 1,300 feet, "where we saw lantern fish, hatchet fish, hake, prawns, and squid," he reported, "but then Wes spotted an octopus through his viewing porthole; I could not see it, so I eased DEEPSTAR around, expecting to see the usual five to six inch warty ball with tiny tentacles, but instead I saw a huge creature. Tentacle to tentacle it probably reached eight feet across, and was the biggest octopus I've ever seen underwater . . . . "

The second monster sighting was also from DEEPSTAR, at a depth of 4,000 feet in the San Diego Trench, off California. Pilot Joe Thompson told the story to Paul Tzimoulis, a Connecticut scuba diver and editor of "Skin Diver Magazine." "I noticed a gray shadow through one of the port side viewports," said Thompson, "then I saw a large eye, as big as a dinner plate . . . . A split second later, I spotted a huge gill plate cover and a two-foot long pectoral fin directly behind it. The great fish appeared to be mottled brown with grayish white tipping of the fin, scales and tail. The gigantic creature was 25 feet long and five feet thick. Unlike the sightings of deep water sharks I've read about, this fish was covered with scales, the largest of which were toward the front; they were about the size of a coffee cup. If you compare the size of the fish to DEEPSTAR'S 6-foot passenger compartment, you can best appreciate how I felt at sighting this incredible beast.... The visual impact was one of watching a long speeding freight train. As it passed, I was able to catch a good view of its thick tail. It was very strange looking, with ragged caudals jutting off its end on a 30 degree angle. It was not the tail of a sea bass or shark," concluded Thompson, "but prehistoric in appearance."

One of the deep sea fish dredged up by the research vessel GALATHEA was a "brotulid" - an aggresive denizen of the abyss - living at about 20,000 feet. It looks something like a codfish in size and shape, but its head is bigger and its body more tapered. It has only slits for eyes; one was caught in the Bay of Biscay, in 1980, that had no eyes. The brotulid is not related to the cod, but another deep water creature is, a strange looking fish called the "rat-tail." It measures about three feet in length, and somewhat resembles the brotulid. At times, marine biologists have mistaken them for each other. The rat-tail however, has large eyes and has a barbel hanging from its chin. It has a body that glows in the dark, and derives its name from its tapering body, which ends in a long filament-like tail. Marine biologists now believe that the brotulid and the rat-tail may be the most common fish in the abyss. I wonder if these two fish, one that looks like a cod, and the other that is related to it, might taste as good as the cod? No one, of course, has tried to eat them and they, as far as I know, have not taken a bite of human flesh-although they might yet prove my father's conviction that the cod is the most dangerous fish in the sea. If they are found to be good eating, their names will have to be changed for brotulid is hard to pronounce (and doesn't sound appetizing) and I'll be damned if I'll ever eat anything called "rat-tail" for dinner.

America's greatest fishing ground is George's Bank, and beyond that, the Continental Slope, which eases down to the great deep, far off the New England Coast. Here live the strange glowing creatures, hundreds of thousands of them, of varying shapes and sizes, yet to be seen by man. These marvelous monsters await the courageous explorers of inner space who are willing to challenge the nightmarish twilight zone called the abyss.

About the Author

Bob Cahill, a native of Salem, Massachusetts, has also resided for awhile in Marblehead and Boston, Massachusetts; Providence, Rhode Island; and Hartford, Connecticut; His wife, Sandy Howard Cahill, is from Keene, New Hampshire. Bob is a former state representative and High Sheriff of Essex County, Massachusetts, and is a graduate of Boston University's School of Public Communications. He was a professional diver from 1954 through 1961, and, for eleven years, was an advertising and public relations specialist for major companies in Hartford and Boston. He served two years as an officer on Army-Security-Intelligence, in Ethiopia, East Africa, where he introduced scuba diving in the Red Sea area, and instructed the Ethiopian Commando Corps in the science of scuba diving. He is a former director of the Massachusetts Board of Underwater Archaeology.

Bob Cahill is the author of a book on diving adventures, "Diary Of The Depths," published by Dorrance & Company of Philadelphia, and co-author of the National Geographic Society's book, "Undersea Treasures." He has written numerous articles on the sea and undersea, and on New England history for such publications as: Yankee, Skin Diver, Boston, Pictorial Living, Ocean Industry, Dive, Saga, and New England Outdoors magazines; and, for The Hartford Courant, Boston Herald, Boston Advertiser, Boston Globe, Salem Evening News, Lynn Item, Lynn Sunday Post, and North Shore Sunday newspapers